Brilliant Bees

By Katy Meeuwissen
Illustrated by Jovan Carl Segura

Library For All Ltd.

Library For All is an Australian not for profit organisation with a mission to make knowledge accessible to all via an innovative digital library solution.
Visit us at libraryforall.org

Brilliant Bees

First published 2021

Published by Library For All Ltd
Email: info@libraryforall.org
URL: libraryforall.org

This book was made possible by the generous support of the Education Cooperation Program and the University of Canberra.

Original illustrations by Jovan Carl Segura

Brilliant Bees
Meeuwissen, Katy
ISBN: 978-1-922721-08-2
SKU01783

Brilliant Bees

Bees are buzzing in the bush.

One bright, busy bee.

Interesting fact

There are more than 20,000 species of bees all over the world.

Two antennae for feeling or sending signals, sounds and smells.

Interesting fact

The bee's antennae can detect vibrations.

Thorax

Head

Abdomen

Three body parts make up the bee. The head, the thorax and the abdomen.

Interesting fact

Bees are insects. All insects have three body parts.

Four wings to help them fly.

Interesting fact

Bees can beat their wings up to 200 times per second. This is what makes the buzzing sound!

Five eyes for seeing sweet smelling flowers.

Interesting fact

Bees can see all colours except red.

Six legs for carefully collecting pollen.

Interesting fact

A bee's body and legs are covered in lots of fine fuzzy hair.

Bees collect pollen to pollinate our plants.

Interesting fact

Bees live in hives or colonies.

They also make honey.

Yum!

Beautiful black bustling bees buzzing in the bush!

You can use these questions to talk about this book with your family, friends and teachers.

What did you learn from this book?

Describe this book in one word.
Funny? Scary? Colourful? Interesting?

How did this book make you feel when you finished reading it?

What was your favourite part of this book?

download our reader app
getlibraryforall.org

About the author

Katy Meeuwissen is a teacher who specialises in Early Childhood and primary education, working in the ACT directorate. Katy is currently working at the University of Canberra, teaching people to become teachers. Katy loves to teach children to read, write, learn and play.

Did you enjoy this book?

We have hundreds more expertly curated original stories to choose from.

We work in partnership with authors, educators, cultural advisors, governments and NGOs to bring the joy of reading to children everywhere.

Did you know?

We create global impact in these fields by embracing the United Nations Sustainable Development Goals.

libraryforall.org

Lightning Source UK Ltd.
Milton Keynes UK
UKHW020900271021
392877UK00007B/158